HOW AWESOME CAN YOU BE?

BE TRUSTWORTHY

by Sloane Hughes

Consultant: Beth Gambro
Reading Specialist, Yorkville, Illinois

BEARPORT PUBLISHING

Minneapolis, Minnesota

Teaching Tips

Before Reading

- Look at the cover of the book. Discuss the picture and the title.
- Ask readers to brainstorm a list of what they already know about being trustworthy. What can they expect to see in this book?
- Go on a picture walk, looking through the pictures to discuss vocabulary and make predictions about the text.

During Reading

- Read for purpose. As they are reading, encourage readers to think about trustworthiness in their own lives.
- Ask readers to look for the details of the book. What are the specific ways someone can be trustworthy?
- If readers encounter an unknown word, ask them to look at the sounds in the word. Then, ask them to look at the rest of the page. Are there any clues to help them understand?

After Reading

- Encourage readers to pick a buddy and reread the book together.
- Ask readers to name two ways to be trustworthy that are included in the book. Go back and find the pages that tell about these things.
- Ask readers to write or draw something they learned about being trustworthy.

Credits:
Cover and title page, © Kraig Scarbinsky/iStock; 3, © annebaek/iStock; 5, © Monkey Business Images/Shutterstock; 6, © kool99/iStock; 8–9, © Kostikova Natalia/Shutterstock; 10–11, © SDI Productions/iStock; 13, © Studio Romantic/Shutterstock; 14, © Monkey Business Images/Shutterstock; 16, © djmilic/iStock; 17, © VioletaStoimenova/iStock; 18, © Chimpinski/iStock; 19, © JGA/Shutterstock; 20–21, © FatCamera/iStock; 22TL, © SerrNovik/iStock; 22TR, © New Africa/Shutterstock; 22BM, © SouthWorks/iStock; 23TL, © monkeybusinessimages/iStock; 23TR, © LightFieldStudios/iStock; 23BL, © SDI Productions/iStock; 23BM, © SDI Productions/iStock; and 23BR, © PeopleImages/iStock.

Library of Congress Cataloging-in-Publication Data

Names: Hughes, Sloane, author.
Title: Be trustworthy / by Sloane Hughes.
Description: Minneapolis, Minnesota : Bearport Publishing Company, [2023] |
Series: How awesome can you be? | Includes bibliographical references and index.
Identifiers: LCCN 2022031852 (print) | LCCN 2022031853 (ebook) | ISBN
9798885093262 (library binding) | ISBN 9798885094481 (paperback) | ISBN
9798885095631 (ebook)
Subjects: LCSH: Trust--Juvenile literature. | Reliability--Juvenile literature. | Etiquette for children and teenagers--Juvenile literature.
Classification: LCC BJ1500.T78 H84 2023 (print) | LCC BJ1500.T78 (ebook)
| DDC 170.84/2--dc23/eng/20220810
LC record available at https://lccn.loc.gov/2022031852
LC ebook record available at https://lccn.loc.gov/2022031853

For more information, write to Bearport Publishing, 5357 Penn Avenue South, Minneapolis, MN 55419.

Contents

Awesome to Be Trustworthy

A good friend is there for others.

We all need people we can count on.

Being trustworthy is awesome!

Being trustworthy means keeping your word.

You do the things you say you will.

When you do, people start to trust you.

Keeping your **promises** builds trust.

Tell your friend you will help them.

Then, do it.

That makes you an awesome friend!

Show you are trustworthy by being **honest**.

Always tell the truth.

People know you mean what you say.

When you play a game, follow the **rules**.

Then, people will want to play with you.

You are trustworthy!

Sometimes, being trustworthy is hard.

You want to talk about a surprise party.

But you were trusted to keep the **secret**.

Shh!

Trust builds over time.

You do what you say you will.

Then, people know you are trustworthy.

You **earned** their trust.

Usually, trust goes both ways.

You show others they can trust you.

And you can trust them, too.

You can be awesome.

Being trustworthy is just one way to do it.

Show everyone they can count on you!

Showing You Are Trustworthy

Build trust by playing a game with a friend.

1. Pick jobs. One person is the walker. The other person is the guide.

2. Have the walker close their eyes.

3. Have the guide help the walker safely move through the space.

4. Switch jobs!

Glossary

earned achieved for work done

honest truthful

promises things people have said they will do

rules guides for how things should be done

secret something only a few people know

Index

Read More

Armentrout, David. *Let's Be Honest (Being Your Best).* New York: Crabtree Publishing, 2022.

Hughes, Sloane. *Count On Me: How to Build Trust (Life Works!).* Minneapolis: Bearport Publishing, 2022.

Learn More Online

1. Go to **www.factsurfer.com** or scan the QR code below.
2. Enter "**Be Trustworthy**" into the search box.
3. Click on the cover of this book to see a list of websites.

About the Author

Sloane Hughes is a writer living in New York. They have written many books for children and young adults.